A Prism for the Sun

Rose Flint

Oversteps Books

First published in 2015 by

Oversteps Books Ltd
6 Halwell House
South Pool
Nr Kingsbridge
Devon
TQ7 2RX
UK

www.overstepsbooks.com

Printed in Great Britain by imprint digital, Devon

for all my family

Acknowledgements:

Many thanks to The Arts Council, South West who supported the Kingfisher Project in Salisbury District Hospital and Salisbury Arts Centre for so long. Thanks to the ArtCare team and everyone at SAC, and particular thanks to Catherine Sandbrook, Peter Ursem and Gemma Okell whose vision and belief enabled so much poetry. And thanks to all the Kingfisher Poets, past and present for their words.

With thanks to the Friends of the Royal United Hospital, Bath, and Hetty Dupays for her encouragement and support. Thanks to Eleanor Glover whose beautiful artwork of Elements of Healing is on permanent display at the RUH.

Many thanks to the editors of the magazines Scintilla, Poetry Review, Resurgence, The Rialto and Artemis where some of these poems were first published, and to the editors of the anthologies: Elements of Healing, Lapidus, James Hogg at 80, Poetry Salzburg.

Marking China Blue was highly commended in the Poetry on the Lake competition, 2014.
Six uses for Scratched CDs and old Tapes: Scarecrow was commended in the Second Light competition, 2014.
Accidental Shadows and *Song of You* were commended in the Charles Causley competition, 2013.
The Tenderness of Men was highly commended in the Second Light competition, 2011.
Reciprocal was short-listed for the Bridport poetry competition, 2008.

Contents

Elements of Healing

Sparrowhawk by the bird table

A shivering absence of small bodies
who'd slant sun rain across brown feathers, scurry,
quarrel, dip over seedheaps, some bread. No robins
singing domestic arpeggios in the tower of the bay tree,
no wren in the tunnel-hides of broken lavender,
no bright ones, longtail, coal and blue, fire, green
gold making dry fennel stalks and new shoots flutter.
Now too still.

        Sparrowhawk is parting the grey lavender
with hard yellow eyes, checking out winter desiccation
with his yellow talons, listening with blood for blood.
          He tramples. Fiercely dances.

His intent sets him apart from scattered dunnocks
who seem like infants caught hard against a warlord
and I worry and love them, those little ones.
        Yet I burn for this vivid barbarian,
this splinter of violence flown into the garden
like a thrown knife, dagger in meat, ring-jewelled fist,
blued wings a cape of trophy skins, honed gaze
a thousand miles. This morning his cold eye is all hawks,
all falcons, great eagles gyring steeple heights of white air
ascending over dumb bloodied bones in heather.

What in me leaps to him, wants him, chooses
beyond his solitary beauty and finesse? His shine –
metallic thread in the weaving of finch, seed, Spring?
Or that recognition he brings, heart-shock, timely?

He is structure to hold the song. He is shadow and scythe
setting each moment of wild light flying in glory.

You at the bird table, sun-up

Would you be St Francis? Be still long enough
to let birds alight along your shoulders, open arms?
They are as slight as kisses and as patient.
Close in the chestnuts, gold epaulettes
flash under green, chaffinches huff red, pause
as you reach up awkwardly against the bitter wind
and scatter seeds across the makeshift board
beneath the kitchen window. I'm washing cups again,
watching your ritual of morning gifts.

Something in you that's good and beautiful
makes your gestures sacred: offering and prayer.
Beyond gentleness, attending to small hungers,
you are binding the bright song-book through
this sharp March garden of sombre hedges
and shut windflowers, into summer dawns
when we will wake too early and find ourselves
afloat like angels in the hour of the great half-dark,
a cathedral of music arching around us
in leaves of air and joy –

                    the hour when the Herald
calls the soul to love unreservedly, climbing up high,
opening the heart to this note and this – each song
a vivid wing – coral, cyan – a prism saved for the Sun
to flood rapture through every life, every beginning.

Pheasant stalking carefully

Pheasant cockles softly, our lawn silver-early,
white filling this pre-dawn air, even to the spaces
between grass-blades, between bird and pole,
between the willow's bud-braided yellow ropes.
This April morning is blurred glass. Sun
as Magician, waiting for the moment: timing is all.
He develops excitement in daffodils, shook goldleaf
starring hedges, edges of fields over there, west.

Pheasant is as intricate as Manchuria,
coloured smooth fable of burnt umber, sheens
of copper, bronze lattice. That green malachite throat
polished, ruby finished, oiled metallic poured sheen.
His snow collar is priestly, his feet finick
dubiously in the wet. That small black eye is troubled:
How can I be? he asks. *All this structure of cells*
for understanding forests and mountains,
for the verdant applause of nymphoides,
ginseng, myrtle, original nasturtium.
I am born a million sons out of my skin –

We soothe him with safety of sunflower and bread
but he runs: even the grass is incomprehensible,
only the sunrise, nested in deep leaves, is home.

Flocks

It's the grace of them I miss,
rushing over my head unconcerned and singing –
as if they accepted my presence and joy in them
as ordinary as gorse bush or hawthorn tree.

Rare now to see charms of goldfinch
alight like bonfire sparks on dry fennel,
or a long brown ploughed field fill suddenly
with chequered semaphores of lapwings
green as crested waves until they lift
and rise – flaring black and white.

How is the emptying world for birds
that once flew in tumbled flocks of hundreds?
There is no shield against the wind, no
wisdom songs, no safe community of others.

Every day that Earth dwindles into ruled lines
and single colours, the flocks grow smaller, fading out.
In my garden, a single fieldfare lingers with the apples;
beyond the fence, redwings swoop across the beets
in little handfuls, and on the ancient marshes
someone's taking pleasure shooting swans.

Looking for Little Egrets

Three once, in the wet meadows nearby.
Three together, ornamenting a skeleton elm
thistledown delicate as snowblossoms

caught on a spike of bone. One I saw
accompanying a grey heron to a morning oak
leaning over a rivulet; a white fairy bird

with a suncatcher beak, goldblade, piercing flash –
weeks later, white feathers in the dark
underhedge, a round of blood soakaway.

Out here, in this Eastland, waterland edge
seamarsh for miles, little egrets become
possible again. Small flares here and there

lighting the flatness; solitary,
dipping the estuary on elegant legs.
Something about their fineboneness.

The how of their making so precise
and surprising, the why – some kind of gift?
A fragment of a story beyond all this

land and water, these creeks and farms –
their whiteness: something angelic
could be as vulnerable to incomprehension

that would separate soul from flesh
with one unthought act – or wholly seen
offer this lift of light heart, spirit-blessing.

Afternoon, a spit from the road

At first, Stag and Raven are present slight as spirits –
in the waver of leaves in high pines where one bird
resettles claws, shuffles shoulder feathers
blue as ink; in red that shimmers briefly behind
tall wet-silver can't-go-there-grass.

Moss patches sit comfy and green-eyed
as clusters of cats under threads of briar.
I can almost hear the feral hiss of disturbance
as I clump through paths fraught with a trickery
of snappy sticks, frail leaf litter. Here, I am big
as a Percheron and my old sweetheart hound
is panting like a flappy banner proclaiming:
We are here! Not what I want to say.

But we can settle under;
cover sound tracks with enough approximation
of silence to begin the letting go of edges and separation.
Easier are days when Wind blusters about in the larches
like a bully kid out of school, banging and shoving air
into thick blocks or tatters that muffle our traces,
our hot human odours. Today, we crouch beside stumps
under black half shadow, still into quiet, waiting
for Wood to re-make itself round us, take us in.

We are only a spit from the road:
this overgrown spinney on the edge, the between
of fields, lanes, bridle paths peaty dark as soaked leather.
Green light filters down from the tops of spidery beeches
through old coppicing, abandoned pheasant feeders,
edges the grace of sweet chestnuts full-skirted as brides.
Green light, black shadows, ferns brilliant
in cut emerald fractals. Rare sun this summer;
not since bluebells hazed everywhere with a colour
more loving even than sky. I fell into bluebell drift
like a swimmer in twilight. Lost everything.

Stag and Raven. Down at the farm they tell me
there are no ravens here. I get pitying looks, as if
I was talking of transplanted choughs from South Stack.
I won't mention the three Little Egrets the foxes took,
nor the single stork I glimpsed by the rail track.
But I walk here under Scots Pines and listen to Raven's
hundred voices, feel the black rough royal shadow
criss cross the heights, swoop over the calves' field
to the fence, back again, asking: *Why? Who are you?*
I answer as best I can.

Midsummer the stags are patina'd rose goldleaf
and prancing. We sit surrounded by hazy scents
of pale stinkhorn, rot, loam – and Stag looms delicately
out of the bracken, making the wood an arena for display,
his arias braggart as any tenor or even the lions
in the next valley whose breath comes like thunders
in the starred clouds of winter's 4 am.
Stag is true prince in residence. I've seen him
dance on his own, practicing his enticements
of little rushes and jumps, his growling song and bark.
He has frightened me at night with his maleness and threat,
his candelabra of sharpened antlers.

Goosegrass, cranesbill, dog rose; stacked deadwood sticks
for generation where moths sneak under and spores
form subtle snows. A deer carcass by the fence,
throat gone; badger sets; thick-furred russet fox
clenched on rabbit – this is Wildwood at the field's corner;
existing haphazardly, as it has grown, intricate
without any grandeur, its own order encompassing whatever
chooses to root here. And the whole green-meshed song of it,
is one tiny molecule of the great beating heart of the wild
that lives always close to us: close as our own forgotten soul.

Telling her death

I went to tell the wood, the deer, and Raven –
but Raven already knew
and responded from the tip of a fir
his voice resonating through the still air
harsh and fast. *She was Beauty* he says.
Golden Hound. Celebrate.

The deer were absent until I chose to walk deep
to a mossed log above the steep fall of the valley,
a thin brackish stream below and sudden ferns.
Then the does lazed to their feet,
threading through bracken and hazel, half-spirit,
half-seen. Death is always as close to them
as their pelt, this is a culling-ground,
always in season, for trees, for deer, for the lost.

We walked slowly here because she was old
and bone-aching. Inside my own story
I'd go too far ahead and she'd lose me
in the dark of her eyes and ears, so we would stop,
let the wood enclose us, hold us. She'd sit
beside me watching light, for hours.

We made such slow journeys through
our heart's geography. I make them still.

The consolation of birds

All this week the oak trees curved
into greyness, collecting the last of the rain
in their high entreating leaves but losing it
too fast too fast spilling it out on the hard roads,
nothing for roots except dust.

I went out in the storm of confusion,
little foxes in my heart yipping
blood, yipping spoiled torn centres
all fragmented, running over cold fields
with my head in wheat, my hands in barley,
cinder and sand or marshland
under my running, over the grey bank
and the praying trees in the awful wind

until the hawk consoled me
floating over close, mewing: flying cat.
And the magpie who shouts at my early window
offered a sheaf of his silky petrol colours.
Then the ground beneath my feet
presented so many small joys: petal, stamen,
leaf and green – I could not count them

and I began to see how the hill shone
and that I was part of the hill in my own shining,
and the birds were like sparks
on the smoothed dome of the sky.
So then the oaks grew calm again
and applauded us all, their light in fountains.

For my brindle lurcher, Kizzie

Downwind, she teases doe-scents
   from wind's tumbled perfumes – grasses and
vermin, stink-fox, honeysuckle –
   thunderbolts
after deer, would deal death blow after blow, red-
fanged, red-misted
  with the devil of hunt thumping her heart
     enough to go with bravado
   over any barriers of swollen torrents
or hazards of rock and thicket –
       She doesn't leap but imagines herself
         through dwarf tunnels that deer thread
secretly into spiked hedges, gashed fences
     goes under and fails, so she is torn,
lacerated, broken
    and only then, after losing time
and fleeting odours, she tears free and turns
   to find me, comes smiling;
    her warhound mind dazzled
       breath and eye still part of the wild.

Or on the beach she races so fast
she is joy of sun scattering a wave,
her speed a dark star, all delight. Swims out
in big tides, her head small as a seal-baby
dot in all that unending grey ocean.

At night she comes softly to rest her long face
in my hands, serious with sleep
and innocent of all harm. She simply
loves. Curls beside me, loose-boned.
I watch her dream processions
of hares and roebucks under big moons
where she is forbidden, so she runs the silverland
in her sleep; a Gabriel Hound, a nightmare,
vocal as birds, or wolf, throat-singing.

I know no one else so paradoxical
and wish my own heart could hunt so straight
to cull and come so carefree into trust.

Near night, July

My young hound is rushing ahead too fast
over the green near-night fields, too fast
for the sudden buck who leaps from the hedge
and races, twists and swerves
cornered at the field's edge so my heart stops
but they are off again too fast
past the line of the covert out through the maize
two swift grey shadows running –

I should call her back –

but she won't come. She must stretch her limbs
out to the limit, test her strength here in the place
that's nearest to wild, these cut hay-meadows
and fields of green corn still pale in the darkening.

I should call her back –

I can never remember a July so beautiful.
So little difference between fields and sky
evening sunfall dimming long bars of gold
over blue; night's slowturn towards emerald.
I sit and wait, as white moths spiral over
tiny, dim field-flowers and bats skim the hedges;
an owl *hoos* softly, fox slips past in shadows –
so many dancing perfumes in the warm half-dark.

I should call her back –

But I can't shout, can't shatter this deep quietness.
I have no permission to unsettle the silence
of life out here, living/dying on one turn of a leaf.
I can't fracture this stillness of rustling songs
that nettles and bracken make. I can only wait

until my dog returns to my tame hands, slumps
obedient with exhaustion, her tongue lolling.
So night continues: beautiful killers and flowers,
The land piercingly alive.

Osprey migrating with the moon

He leaves Scotland suddenly, lifting off
from a high pine branch as the sun falls beneath him
and the full moon swells inside his desire for Africa.

He follows the curves of contours and hollows;
farms are sleep-shuttered, only the eyes
of owls and shining lakes, know that he goes.

In Madrid, tourists are crowded in pleasure,
all is *rioja, pata negra, calamares, bacalao* -
guitars lifting, yearning dreams to the dark.

Osprey floats over, finding his silence. He flies on,
and on, across thousands of miles of clear silver sky
because tonight is beautiful around him.

In Andalucía a woman has danced *duende* since dusk,
now she shrugs on her thin black coat, awkwardly,
sleeve snagging. Rhythms shred her heart into wings.

In the small dim hours, a barman lays his cloth
on the counter, snaps out electric candles beside
his life-size, painted Mary. Her eyes still shine.

Osprey flies over steep and plain spread below
like messages; mountains and black rivers all
part of his circling story of memory and bone.

Hot winds come to him laden with birdsongs
crescendo of morning; as I open my window
to watch the sun alight in my street, Osprey

drops softly down into Africa with the moonfall;
goes slow now, home to the greeting egrets
and the beckoning arm of the tree by the creek.

Of all wasps, only hornets fly at night

My terror of this alien midnight flyer hurtling at glass,
falling and climbing and falling on my window,
scattering itself in the ivy; no stars, darkness, and I
inches away, unwillingly fixed: learning the hornet.

I work late into moony silence, grassy air,
one young summer owl calling. I am deep in. Until
sudden shock into danger sweating my leaping spine,
my scrambling lurch for safety. I am furious
at this invasion of *my* night, *my* dark, *my* calm, time
safe from the fear of a random sting that would throw me
again into the heat and heart-rate of anaphylactic shock
too toxic to bear. Two have entered my room.
They are huge, erratic, screaming, itinerant marauders
who have no malign intent, only confusion.

Hornet flings itself hopelessly through the thickened air
terrified by this world of walls, of books and china:
Where is my home under the ivy and jasmine? I am lost.

They are nesting in the roofspace above my head.
Days now, I see them: immense, intent, gold-brown,
floating out slow at first, then speeding, zig-zagging.
Soon they will be disbanding, dying, hungry
for sugars, searching – day and night with us.
I can't live beside them.

Before the man comes I make a vigil for them –
some honouring with attention – guilt or reparation.
There are more now, swarming over black glass,
their voices raised angrily at the light's trickery,
antennae pulsing, delicate feet slipping and scrabbling,
leaving tracks. I am repulsed by their keen yellow heads
but their sheer force awes me; they seem huge, lion-creatures
filled with terrible, impersonal fury. And I hate them
for the fear they bring me, which makes me
a lesser person than I thought I was, takes me down
to sheer survival: killer instinct – that force we always use
to place ourselves at the emptying summit of creation.

After the Planning Meeting

This Town had a purpose towards joy.
It sat quietly thinking at the edges of meetings
listening to new ideas for urban planning
and the knowledge – serious as great bells –
of right living. This warmed the Town's heart.
How, after threadbare times and makeshift
some integral caring could arise in its place.

So the river could cease sickening
and be brought back to health; working out,
turning energy, giving its bright ions
and light to dragonflies and joggers
or those stumblers who are confounded by wonder
and stutter along paths beside shining
telling the children to love it all: flow, tumble, flood.

The Town's wind will grow up, up
catch hold of its power and pass it on,
linking up to the grid. Clever systems
of waste and heat (yours, mine) will spin
ceaselessly, turning in and out on themselves.
Nothing will be lost. All will be remade.

Curved streets and allotments, zones
of serendipity: homes for the real future,
houses working for a living. And beyond
these tons of strong structures, *wood, glass,*
stones, straw, fleece beyond this mind of strong will,
still the town has a purpose towards joy: hopes
for dancing dresses of cherry trees lining the High Street,
frilled white blossom in Springtime, birds singing
good dreams in the leaves, red fruits for harvest,
street party celebration at the turning year,
town mouths stained luscious with cherry kisses.

Swifts over town

These summer days, I am too open to sky variations,
threats of weather I can't understand: *somewhere
coming close a grey rolling thunder, a flood...*

Sree...sree.... say the swifts. Two, three maybe.
Repeating parabolas of medieval arcs and rooftrees
they chisel the air so fast it falls into the town as dust
moth-winged, spangled on stones.
Where are the others? The sky at the river is bare,
all air a sheet of plain silver, no etchings scored
with their burin screech.

I'm walking in my small-town street
and the sun is kindly so this water, running
in its channel through pavement is shining
like good news and the children dip in fingers
and feet, skin tasting the cool, the free sparkle
rush of it – how it is now.

I count every drop against sand.

Nights, big sky over the field, stardragons
brief crimson flares, enough for astonishment.
What will fall away is the old paradigm,
concrete and painful, shutting us in.
Children of these children will hold swifts
in their hands and release them on some other
tomorrow into the new, right weather –
that we'll make with the answers we give back
to the questioning birds, to water, to sky.

Six uses for scratched CDs and old tapes: Scarecrow

I built her as a conductor of winds and birds.
A fetch, freaking out overweight pigeons,
she is sturdy with chestnut, decent
with my old Foale and Tuffin jacket
that I couldn't bear to junk, and stands gyring,
a glittering shaman loaded with silver eyes,
watching for feathers and weather,
fierce over my Pak Choy and radishes.

She is strung with power
bought with the coin of her flashing glances,
spinning light as lace, sun or rain a *largesse*
or a lightning bolt and all the time she hums
in her silence: Sigur Rós floating over lettuce,
Puccini lifting up under apple shadow.
Yesterday, she had Led Zeppelin hitting
the westerlies behind the calabrese, achieving
the exit of crows. Today, blackbirds stutter
beneath the shivering threads of the Scarlatti
I wound round our gooseberries and she tremors
the breeze with my scratched, beautiful Tallis
that the lurcher played to destruction.
She vibrates Whiskey in the Jar and I drink to her,
Chablis on the lawn watching all the little beans
climbing up under the shelter of La Mer.

But towards dusk, I won't catch her eyes
when they turn white and full of reflection.
I won't encourage her to up-sticks and stump off,
wandering out into the maize to scare rooks
and stray children with a tintinnabulation
of straw, trailing red nasturtiums and The Pogues.

This family

One son, once an architect of glass towers
estranged from knowledge of grass or paths
began making the first hieroglyphs
for hanging cities in air, so they could sway
like panniers on the round backs of rearing tornadoes
arriving wild-eyed. Systems funnelled
all stormy weather; music on good days,
so saxophones still played sundowning streets
plangent with all that jazz.

A daughter has taken a stand on top of the world,
found carved words in ice.
She reads them through atmospherics,
through thin rings of electricity, through veils
of green auroras, through ancestry.
She has won a circle sacred as any prayer wheel:
wilderness for white foxes, marine gene-pool.
No sea roads, only the dark re-breeding sea.

Father hosed down his neighbour's house
when the fire came, breathing black.
Now he has trained himself in the tricks of fire-sticks
taking brands from the sun to temper the forest,
let new shoots grow like fur.
His houses lean into hot winds across ditches
and breakers, old trees, wet-leaved come close;
so we all sleep safe under shush of branches.

And Mother? She works as always.
She has rolled up the carpets of lawn around her,
transformed old acres sleek as soft jade.
Her huge hands sift down gardens of bean trees,
seeds of melissa, yellow squash, blue corn.
She has pushed ten kinds of vine into every crevice
so fruitfall and seeds rootle into the year.

The family has seen the mountain stumble into the lake,
fire burn theatres and stables, sea consume the shanty,
wind lay waste the song of tomorrow's birds.
The family is smaller now, but daily grows fierce
in love and invention. Everywhere, we are listening
to water, learning from earth, conserving all solar traces,
our breath in unison rising in a clear new song.

The Frozen Ark

where the DNA of endangered species is being stored

Nested vials in cloudy cold, row on row of species
sleeping curled into the single speckle
of their DNA. Our Keeper ranks them tier on tier:
over here, the big cats caught before they faded
to a rumour stalking dreams. I could place them
on one hand: Sumatran Tiger reeking
of the swampland, Saudi Lioness with her eyes
of pale lemon moon. Here, beside the top joint
of my little finger sits the anorexic cheetah
and the great black jaguar, whose silent coming
roared such spirit thunder it tied a tribal vision
to the land. And look, on my thumb a single mark
of rosette-printed snow leopard, whose long
ancestral memory seems complicit with this ice.

Count these freckles on my skin and name them:
little margay, lynx and caracal, highland wildcat,
Golden Cat of Africa that graced the midnight forest
and the chieftain's robes. Iriomote, ocelot and puma,
felis margarita – I hold all these and more.

And will they come back, ever? Will the centuries
roll towards a time when we'll afford the grace
of empty tracts of land: no wheatfields, war-zones,
cities, no mines for rare earth elements or fuel?
Will the cats come stepping slowly
from their clouds of freezing mist, staring
at the way we've engineered another Eden –
a brand new wilderness to which we make no claim?

Snow day celebration

Sudden big snow, a whiteout of air
and everything changes as elation
leaps out of memory accepting again
this present: all this unexpected light.

Trees are silver branches feathered with sugar,
vane, rachis and barb in crystal;
the white map of the lawn is drawn
with the country of wildness come closer:
crow-tracks and badger, the small careful prints
of a fox, hopeful right to the door.

At the station, schoolgirls build snowmen
on freezing iron seats and their Dad
wields a blue shovel over the platforms.
We all wait patiently,
watch the clock pass departure time, on and on.
I think of the train as courageous, heroic,
bravely battling the weather to reach us,
doing its best as some great-hearted horses would do:
power harnessed to succour.

Snow's beauty eases temptations to surly mood so
we all smile. Being this cold is new again
is itself another country.
I could be travelling in a fabulous landscape of reindeer
and wolf, past iced lakes secret with kelpies,
treacherous marshes of bitterns and crane,
pure, swan-wing meadows under hill's outlines
chalked on the lucent grey sky.

My toes curl gladly in fleecy boots.
I would rather have these freezing moments
for all their disarray and chaos, would rather shiver
than lose this sight of those few slow lapwings
lifting their chequered wings up from the snow,
drawing whole continents closer together.

Winter solstice

A day that is apparently dull grey.
People shake the thin rain from their hands
as wetness slides into the cracks of shoes
under the collar, in through the sleeve.
The town huddles   not glad.
            It is the darkest day.

Out on the hill the long slow night
is coming in with mist white softness.
Already edges are blurring and the valleys float;
        in rills and springs the water sings
            so much rain
black leaves shine like steel
sharps on the grass   trees are black sticks
            so much rain

Soon the darkness will lie down here,
cover the sprinting hare, the sleeping heron.

The light will still work for you.
It is slipping down quietly through the roots
of trees, through the dreams in the skull
of the hare and the heron,
through the metalled leaf's decay on the grass.

    Light and water and night
are all one. All are the falling star
still travelling towards the solstice.

Tonight there will be a moment
when nothing will breathe.
We will reach the resting point, the deep
        fulcrum of the year

            and the light will pause

then send its thin pale fires out
into the heart of everything
        and begin again to rise.

Reciprocal
i.m. Edmund Cusick

That night, the white owl loved me enough to wait
in the smoky laurels beyond the door
starlight describing winter psalms in leaf-lines
around him, the saying of late January scribbled on ivy-darks
and shadows; black land held fast, a waste of iron and ice

and the white owl – *white only*
in his decisive collection of light, the way he pulled it
under his fringed mottled brown wings
such a snowfall to confuse in silent mothy flight –
a tawny, soft-voiced for weeks between the great oaks
and the little bare cherry, waited on a branch. So:
he was there when I took my fury out to confront
the deep sky with its arms wide open reaching down to me
that flooding implacable zodiac of joy;
my ears ringing, eyes rivers.

I was trying to locate you somewhere between Sirius
and Rigel, while Auriga blazed as fiercely
as any remembered death does in the first world-blind weeks.
The emptiness of blue frosted days arched more greatly
in their unlettered hours; there was no poetry.

No ghost bird, but pearl-pale, he watched me, from low down
in the smoky laurel – *once I gave your daughter owl-whistles*
to call them through the dark. Once we stood still long enough
to allow sun and moon both to roll along our shoulders.
Why do I grieve? I knew
you would let the flower-faced goddess open any gate.

I do not know if I touched something
in the mind of the owl. It was as if he was experimenting
with my humanness, testing, taking time.
But there was nothing more momentous on that freezing night
than his communion: he offered the wake and the song
gathered gently at last from between the breastbone
and the heart, a handful of flung stardust, chimes.

Blue early

Thirsty, rising sun laps up
early frost, leaving warm violet
shadows under the hedge

dreams disturbed my sleep
so I went out hunting for myths
while the world seemed unwritten enough
for any story to happen.

Through the kissing gate, alone,
my face cold – under the strake of willows
restless chequer of vipers
in their tight hard hanging buds

down to the river, surly and dark at this hour,
private under alders frowning blackly
keeping night close about them
here or nearby.

I'd walk out of this morning
into the next
follow the wood's line, stepping soft as a fox,
for a sighting of something so joyous
it told me a story I want to belong in.

We all want blaze and certainty, the rightness
of tomorrow, the way the story arcs heroically
to promise and reward
but even the wood
can offer nothing of the future of oak and ash

only show me these moments of blue now

all else falls away.
It is enough to love again, like the first day.

The way stone excites me enough to sing

For piezoelectric cells to shift quartz time
for electromagnetic energy confusing prosaic needles

for mica and its interest in starlight
for storm-blueness in slate, lake-blue in serpentine

for granite's peculiar weightlessness that may dance
when dusk or dawn is aware, that may hustle to the river

on folkloric nights. For my past life, grooving messages
in abstract, helios in the dark under, flaring light

for stone's fist, its heft, its clear shout – flint splintering
into components of violence or domesticity

for its font, lion-face, angel, idol,
for its calm gold holy faces, ascending prayer

for its earrings and brooches, doves of rhodocrosite
that coo softly to you over supper,

for its diamond on my daughter's finger
its deep silver ooze, for its opal refracting the weather

for its secret crystalline places, its caves of the mind
its sheer slopes of moonlight

for its mountain – canyon climbing in terror
and that red rock glowing fired ruby at 3 am

for its descent, its shift and survival
for its minutia of thought, slowness of scarp

into clay into china that I lift to my lips to celebrate
everything so ordinary where I stand

between solid home ground and the radiant stars
clustered over like a beach of bright pebbles.

Circus Skills for Young Girls

for Nancy Rose

How to speak mountain and police.
How to wake before words, how to build fires
from ash, brew bitter leaves and befriend
the Strongman whose chest is tattooed
with sharks and mermaids, crying.
How to tear fishnet, use silver,
achieve muscles like hawsers under silk
green and fine as the turn of the tide.
How to practise Dream.
How to lie when your arm is twisted.
How to run in the dark without drowning.
How to wash with moonsoap in a pail of silence.

How to dive.

How to learn the tricks and hooks of roads
and dry towns. How to tend chimeras
and power; how to build one-minute myths
from the huge scissor leaps of your legs –
how to elude the hobble of midnight binding.
How to reach Cassiopeia and the spangles,
go higher than Saturn or Mars, go higher,
kicking water, swallowing heat, soaring
through blue nightingale evenings of adoration,
with dark tinsel wings and lungs on fire.

How to always remember how to fly.

All the horses are gifts

for Nancy Rose

I'd want you to know horses.
So if you were dancing on the broad table-back
of a ribbon-tailed piebald, huge as oak,
hardly disturbing the sawdust so smooth he goes –

it would comfort me with a history of Falabella
in a garden, soft as velvet
    and your little face pressed close.
        Or early in frost, breathing in
the meadow-breath of a bay racehorse,
seventeen hands tempered to speed.

I'd want you to know standing in the dark
to call the name that brings the wild mare
shining like gentian, to lisp her soft mouth
across your fingers. I'd teach you to whistle
to the great starry Percherons of my childhood,
let you weave through their quiet legs, brush
their massive quarters, lift up their unshod hooves
which could kill you with no more than a flick.
I'd want to take you down the dangerous path
through the woods to the sandline where the roan
kicks water into fountains, lets go all his joy.

I'd want you to enter the place of risk and trusting
all that is Other: horses and trees, the star-wheel
and the glittering sea – to learn the great universe
of your own heart's bright compass.

Going with the Magician

for Nancy Rose

If you go to the steep land of wolves
with the Magician, please write

let me know that you are keeping
the mountains in their place

that you still know the origin of roses
and crimson silk, that you recognise

white doves and breakfast eggs and don't
only eat gold beans and smoked fish.

Don't talk sadly to Jack-rabbit
who is fake and sneaky. Search out

the old woman who will not be fooled
(there will be one with my gaze).

Let her see the man, in all his glossy tack,
his smile. He will use his charms on her.

She and I could spell them out for you
although you wouldn't want to read them –

but read her eyes. Remember your own magic
is sacred sun, true ore and if he pulls down

the black velvet sky to wrap you,
places the Pearl of the Crown in your hair

with soft fingertips touches – so you kiss –
and become part of the wild atoms

of the world and you two *are* the universe –
then you will remember nothing I have said

if it is the beginning of the story
that unlocks time. Changes everything.

All the hares in the valley

That day all the hares
came into the valley
where we were lain down in love

only the quick rosy shimmer of larks
disturbing the air
and our noise

where the grass took us in
rolled us over
limbs bare to sunlight

and the hares sat motionless
watching

whatever they thought or said
going through the quiet
moving as the air itself does
moving through everything
like blessing

and we set up such a wave in our grass bed
we shaped a world

with the hares and the larks and the sun itself
always within it.

Girl – this is for when you are splintering

Put images of women everywhere,
ads and art-cards, birthday cards – but all women.
They are all you, and will remind you of who you are,
on the days when you can't really remember.

Put the Mona Lisa by the door, her smile
can say anything that the visitor needs to hear.
Put the Rokeby Venus by your bed;
she really tells you how to get laid,
its in her reflecting gaze. No one will notice
anything else; not your glassiness and hard edges.

Remove the Venus of Willendorf to a safe box
and take out in small doses, to be fat with
or thin with, whichever power is necessary.

I once tried Doris Day in the kitchen thinking
I could fix gingham cupcakes to make myself better,
but my face froze into a grimace that was truly
as terrible as my hairstyle and I ignited the baking
with barely a glance.

Please don't go to Frieda either
she will just make it worse and give you command
over snakes who will follow you about
from a shadow about six feet away, unsettling
the parquet floors like a half-visible game
of snakes and ladders that must be played
every time you cross the hall.

Sometimes, it's in the detail. That naïve artist,
a woman who painted a woman rowing a boat
away from shore, the night fair with moonlight;
she has everything she needs in her bundle.

But always keep something by the back gate
for emergencies: a vintage Leonora Carrington
with catbird, running mandolin, womanhorse,
and a couple of truly wild old ladies, their hair
already going skywards, pointing the way out.

Unforeseen consequences of 60 and on

for Rosie Jackson

You become more reluctant to expose fleshy parts
to the public gaze, even odd ones like knees
which become untrustworthy on every level
so kneeling is utterly proscribed, as is stooping,

so young gardeners are always necessary
preferably the male and ornamental kind
which you can watch from behind sunglasses,
gin and tonic and the fragrant homemade lemon polenta
you have set out on the terrace.

The Senior Railcard is a wild gift,
with occasional refusals by nice guards
who say that your ticket simply can't
belong to you, miss, and you must be cheating.

And the bus pass, whilst delivering free travel
does afford you the chance to keep leaping girlishly
on and off the bus to dive into unsuitable shops
selling things like glitter slippers and balcony bras
which you buy foolishly and gleefully, knowing
that you have saved all that money on fares.

It is possible to be tired and be offered a seat
by a teenager, without her mother poking her.

And you can wear red and swear blind
that you are 40, because of course, you are.
And you can go dancing in high heels that hurt
but make you feel like flying at least until midnight

when you re-enter your usual life
that may centre around the cat, the book,
the comfy bed – or even the gardener
lured in by the scents of Vanilla, Lemon
and Shea Butter Body Scrub Intensive
wafting over the new-mown lawn
and the tidy borders beyond your open window.

The tenderness of men

The ones who are too fierce with their sons
the ones who ignore their daughters
and urge them to marry only
the ones who hate, smouldering in their wing chairs
the ones who fight, drunken lords at 6am
the ones who glide over motorways of whisky and ice
the ones who hurt
the ones who beat bruises under eyes
the soft ones, who cannot speak
the terrified
the ones who sneer, inflict casual wounds
the ones who are malign with neglect, speechless
the cold ones who recite timetables as if to hold
the whole framework of their life: road names,
roundabouts, distances travelled out of unimaginable
mists
the ones who seal-off hope, wall it up
the ones who bank living, never live
the ones who refuse music
the warriors
                    all these, may be tender
in the quiet of their gardens, gaunt thumbs
pricking a seedling, gentling soil from small leaves.
Or they may be stunned to tears and photography
by wildly technicoloured sunsets over the ocean;
all those colours they can't name, but experience
painfully, as if love held them new again, in its big arms.
            As between the seed and the sun the universe
        is strung together, and they too are part of it,
and it is everywhere, flowing with tenderness, even for them.

Bloodlines

My Father's Father, and his, my bloodline,
took the exile-track across the ocean,
a keening wake following so close
it made green waves a map of mountains,
a chart of hungry fields of reeds and iris.

They took fiddles, seeds, summer dances;
turned their church around for travelling,
arched roof and rafters a palindrome
whose deep hold of the heart would keep them
safe beneath the crosstree and the crow's nest.

Soul to soul, candles streaming in the wind.
That light: a storm within the windows
of their eyes, rain or salt or tears coursing
down their faces so when I look
I see them dim and wavering, gazing back
from cloudy silvered underwater mirrors:
no reflection clear enough to claim as kin.

What did they expect from this Immrama?
A paradise of apples, an island rich in palaces
of gold and crystal, demon horses fighting
in the wind? They found a land of frozen trees,
hard winters streaked by red lines in the snow,
alien faces scored with ochre, tattoo blue.
Year on year their dreams of home
became the memoried glens of Tir-nan-n'Og;
the piercing song of longing for return.

Beached, their church still sheltered; pale bones
arched over in a prayer, rubric names settling
into stone, the nave a fierce cradle for new birth.

Welsh church on the hill

It sits in the valley like a boat
half-harboured in ewe pastures
where small oaks are wind-whipped
yellow sails, yearning for calm.

I'd step in to be rocked.
Inside, a good cradling, candled
by red-cheeked angels, smocked
in the comfort of Mary-blue.

But I'd light such a fuse
in this damp October weather
that old Doom would leap from the plaster
shaking his stick like a sacred rattle,
my sour fire and his glee puffing the air
out of the space under the rood.

Grim saints could do battle
for my thin, transient soul. Doom
doing his dance, while snarled dragons
licking my angry aroma, sleeked fast
as porpoises dipping through green weather;
last blood on the water

Oh those two angels in blue dresses
with familiar faces and fey hands.
Would they take me up and hold me
until the Spring came, bowing with light?
They know I am precious cargo and all at sea.

Out there, beyond the wave

Sea has a fretting kindness today
as if it was never angry enough to drown lovers.
It sits, an active old woman
knitting the business of time,
all the intricate stitches of minutes
that go on to make the rolling fabric of the year.
I am only another figment to be woven in.

I seek attention: offer my naming of colour
those saltgreys and underslates – but
it is not enough. I try harder. Remember
Manannán speaking from his height
close to my ear, what he told me.
She nods at that and I jolt back into a memory
I don't know how I possess. My heart hammers
with the vastness of this small stretch of coast
flexing its thin bone against such spaciousness.

Marking china-blue

The waves come china-blue, over and over.
I put my hands in the sea and pull it towards me
all its coldness and weight, its blue
over and over, pulling the wave, my fingers
combing for flames inside this foamy silver
so it falls through my hands into its small rivers;
water braiding light over and over.

This, inside the paper: the heft of my palm scuffs
chalk, I am drawing the china-blue wave
out of the sea, marking for story, aquamarine:

how tides fall through my body so I am rain
laced in the breakers, rolled so small, over and over.
I make a sound – a long o – round as the roll
of the wave and the pastel blurs into a hollow,
a narrow cone, so small   – not like the two surfers
        yesterday, in their huge tracts of curve and flow,
    up again, bodies in wild blue blaze – these
are the still sea waves, endless and quiet

and I can see the turned dark shape inside the light
coming in animal consolation under my hand,
see its heart beating, over and over. This
is how I am returned to love: late day
pale sea, horizon hazed with acres of unknown light.

Song of you

You could be taken ill on a train and lost,
lying patiently still, between fields of blue flax
and these red bullocks, while crowds snake past you

annoyed and hurrying to catch aeroplanes
and late appointments. You could become pale
as porcelain and I would have to keep trying

to stop the leaks with beer and red dates, with quinces
and pecorino. You could go into the snow again
this winter, take the snow on your tongue like a wafer

or sugar, like bitter almond, a gift no one
ever gave you before. You could get up and leave me
in the night. Just go. Leave me to my hot wakefulness

my silence, my empty arms. Or you could stop
tensely putting your hand over your heart
with just one small breath. You'd fall like a palace

and the air would be filled with a glittering dust
of frescoes – *blue angel, lion, goatboy,*
fleck of carmine, scatter of gold –

all the aspects of our bed would splinter
into their six directions and I would have to
breathe them back every night, with remembering.

But you would still be absent. And I
would be so furious I'd stop the deer in their tracks
halt the mean stars, take it out on ash trees

and philadelphus, accusing them all of deceit
loudly and long. I would tear up the wheatfields
of your birthday line by line in my anger –

but they would make a stave, despite my fists
and the song of you would still be written there
lilting and tender and lovely as you are.

Elements of Healing
Angel with glittering hands

They are always coming and we never know them,
the great dark angels with wings as heavy
and cold as winter midnight studded with stars,
with their breastplates of moon. This angel
came to the attic skylight – the house so settled,
quiet – one moment that broad radiant face
was still beyond, gazing in, as if this did not
have to be the place, as if there could be
somewhere else to go – but with dipped head
and huge black wings folded like a diving bird
falling between worlds, came on through
the glass, entering the tall house, coming slowly
down dusty landings and worn stairs
on silent burning feet, slowly descending
to the afternoon kitchen where the mother played
with the boy and the baby, sang to the radio,
so the angel came towards her, glittering, pacing
forward, long beautiful hands reaching out
to take the boy, lifting him smoothly away from
his breath, his bread, his green cat and solar drawings.

Slow with purpose and burden the angel turned,
retracing fiery steps, leaving a haze of dark
shining on everything and the space
where the child had lived. And even though
the mother spun round so fast her blonde hair
stung her eyes, even though she leaped
and flung her arms out blindly – she did not see
the angel come and go, ascending the stairs
with her own boy held tenderly against the breast.

I cannot look at the mother. Nor at the shocked baby
who may have seen something. I don't know.
I am looking at the angel and not understanding.
Is it that the boy's time had been a mistake,
an accidental falling from Heaven
which had to be mended so some innate order
of things could continue? Or was it that his purpose
was two years long, no more, all the resonance
of his life going on forever in his absence, altering
souls, changing futures: a terrible, necessary gift?

Something that loves us

All night he dreamed a dream he could not say.

Waking, clouds poured through the window
in a grey silt, fine-grained as regolith;
he saw that some of it was fragmented sun
sand-bright, sharp –

but inside his thought, only dull tide
reached for him and his skull opened
the flood-gate that allowed the world
to float out, very small,
far away from shore.

Who is it that watches over?
Somewhere, an island took him in
with all the compassion
trees are capable of – rubbing his eyes,
his hands, his tender mouth
with snow, until he opened,
came clean again.

Such a long way from home.
He walked all night and did not sleep
but watched a thin, pared-down old moon
shiver between shadow and sudden brightness
that came gentle as the pearl of seashells
held chanting in his child's hand.

Story, no dramas

I don't get dramas, I get quiet ones,
the ones who can talk – walk sometimes –
bored, getting better, fatalistic
they chat, tell stories: easy, urbane, halting,
reticent, *filled up to here with it.*
Sometimes all they have left is medical jargon
easing the gap between sore and loss,
Latinate syllables they speak as incantations,
prayers to someone beyond the priests
bringing comfort in needles and dreams.
Sometimes incredulous – *where am I?*
Not that they don't know the bird on the wall
or the sound of china but *where am I*
in my body, my self run off in pieces, left anyhow –
in a bin, a furnace –

No RTAs, belated caesareans. Just quiet ones.
The man who grew flatter and flatter, thought I
was his amanuensis, confided his life in short chapters
before his spine totally froze and the cold of his heart
spread like spore. That life: backstreets and Liffy,
gunmen loading the shadows, women as livestock.
His own casual defences: knifing all the way
into the lungs and a stranger wiped out of the street.
He watches for me entering the dim corridor.

No dramas. The way it is. A nurse, new to this life
returns one cold winter evening bringing sweet oils
of rosemary and lavender. Her long hair dipping
into the water, gently she washes the feet of a teacher
dying in cancerous fragments, who, sleepless,
is writing a poem on mathematical graces of stars.

Miracles

This is a place of everyday miracles
that break open all the cells of yesterday,
making tomorrow beautiful.

In white clear light Death's thumbprint
is erased, so Time breathes again,
allowing healing to find
its old, original water-course.

Fixing the broken, fusing the bone,
finding the secret spore, the wild gene,
Medics bend like prayers over patients,
their minds dressed in science,
their hands and eyes tenderly
attendant to miracles as ordinary

as these small singing birds who yearly
find their way across half a world
 – *through wavestorm, fire and war* –
to home in to the hospital courtyard
just as the white star-blossomed tree
begins to dance again.

Accidental shadows

There's a shadow-kit on the wall.
Every tool outlined in its position, no mistakes.
You need to grab the right thing when you run, he said.

Precise, ordered, the shadow board shines
the same way that the white coats splinter light,
make something good of ordinary substance,
make it a force to keep the universe in place:

like the rosary of rubbed beads
that hangs beside the scalpels,
someone's lucky cup balanced on a cabinet edge;
the machines that idle through their Book of Numbers
in this afternoon of rare quiet.
Backstage, this whole department
is prayerful enough to be a convent
of Our Lady of the Bleeding Heart
or Black Madonna of the Broken Mind.

But there is Chaos here. Something invisible, felt,
either a ghost of previous experience
or a foretelling of Saturday night.
A shuffling silvery lion
in the corner of my eye, Chaos
pads between iron beds where cellular blankets
are folded stones too worn for warmth. Later,
blood will run almost silently beside us.

Such tension in stillness. The medic's eyes squint
towards the sunlit window and the road.
He's listening. *The worst*, he says.
You want to know the worst?
I shake my head but he is going to tell me
and I feel the cold he feels, contagion chill as ice.
One of the nurses, a friend, pregnant –
I can hear the sirens too, now, but nothing's moving
except Chaos rippling his muscles. *RTA.*

He went on checking lists methodically –
as his memory-hands did what they could
but couldn't save them; his story shapes to hard details
precious to him, insoluble as crystals on a string.

His eyes flick to the corner where Chaos bares his teeth.
Someone came to talk to us. He didn't take up any offers,
there wasn't time on shifts. *It gets Chaotic here.*
He was fine. He got over it. He went on saving lives.

Elements of healing

Here, they will place a shock of fire on your heart
so your body will remember its living rhythm again,
and how your heart can be warm, when it loves.

They will place exotic liquid chemicals
or someone else's blood in needles and syringes,
pierce your own routes of water, (those blue conduits
roaring with tides and memories, moods of the moon)
and they will sail you to safe shore.

They will catch the air for you, in tubes and soft boxes
transparent as flayed angel's skin
and they will breathe for you, slowly, seriously
kiss you back into life.

On your tongue they will place willow and rosy periwinkle
chalks and six kinds of sugar, wafered like bread,
your body will respond, flesh to flesh, turn away from hurt
to blossom and make new, delicious fruit.

They will allow the cool magic of ether to move you
from days crowded with clawed fears
into a healing night peaceful as old black winter velvet.
Then your spirit will grow strong and lovely as amaryllis
that needed a spell of cold darkness before it bloomed like a star.

Discovering the miraculous body as a drum

What is a broken body in its chemicals and flesh?

What is a body that it knows the invisible
beyond its sequences of skin and sinew, beating heart
beyond its formula of genes and numbers underneath
the atavistic deep response to bonfires, frankincense
or one crow's wing held hard against the optic nerve
to better frame the myths of flying light

What is a body that it cries for death to come early
unless there is ease to its own impossible wholeness
race and shape and flow and sex and awkwardness
beyond the severed spine and broken nerve
beyond the petrified reality of sappy bones
heavy fruits of stone suspended from a slender spirit-tree
weak and strong as weeping willow

What is a body when it discovers itself as a drum
the world tuned to a new acoustic, centred in new space

What is a body that echoes, resonates, re-locates,
makes stereophonic initiation: a seedling sense pushing
out from breakage and decay. Raw at first, in discord
noise scrapes harsh, vibrates fire along the unknown tension
of a timbrel-skin inside the self and sometimes dins
tinnitus ringing through the lymph and blood as if
all arbitrary sound came now with a collected purpose:
to beat into the body, to strike *this this this* primal note –
insistent, purposeful, stridently, determinedly alive

What is the body beyond its sack and pieces, beyond
its secret, aching diffusion, its inchoate random knowledge?

What is a body in the music of its uncountable flame and angel?

In my surgeon's hands

My surgeon is top man, the very best,
so skilled in cuts, the burn of laser's eye,
precision well renowned throughout the west;
a modest man, and not afraid to cry.
His hands' swift certainty slide blade through blood
divide atomic beats that frame my life
but understand that bone and meat and flood
are fused to fire far, far beyond his knife.
His own heart answers mine with tenderness,
he feels the weight of love in my heart's hold:
the morning fox, my daughter's gentleness,
your music lying late on frost and cold –
and knows what honour then, to place his art
in swift due service to my precious heart.

Intensive Care

This room has been slotted in between care wards
most carefully: one side looks towards grass
and the place where rain clears
to light in the early morning,

the other aspect faces walls of night
where sometimes stars flash –
or lanterns, set on the masts of quiet boats.

Machines pray constantly, humming low-voiced.
The air in here is often burdened grey
with weights of grief and the darker stain of hopes
that filter through time longer
than any allotment of hours, any division of moons.

Those who minister here are word-perfect
in all the songs of the body, even those lyrics
that spirit whispers, beyond breath.

X-rays

I am laid bare, peeled to the bone
a tree in winter, all my blossoming
as ephemeral as last summer's roses.

Today I must remember
the truth in things, surface and texture and fold:
my just-washed hair, apple-scented;
my skin cool smooth, with a sometime roughness
as in raw silks where threads make light
break across evenness in beauty;

remember, the way my eyes open to the window
where the bare tree sings with an invisible bird.

Creation writing
for J

Frost on snowdrops, she answers, *excuse me*
I'm negative this week.

We work the theme: discuss the seasonal paraphernalia
of cold and crocuses and early bees, the urgency
of growth, new shoots and scents
beyond unopened windows   *and I dream childishly*
of monsters who inhabit shadow's hollows, underdarks
and traps. I wake in fear. I place tokens of Good
around my room to comfort me – a leaf, a book, a painting
made of blues. I sleep and waking
let my eyes find consolation where they can.
But I feel a terror for the doves
who could freeze to death these sudden chill white nights.

Hoarfrost has thinned her skin to paper, petal-fine;
I remind her that these blackest nights of ice that scald the bone
also kill a host of unwanted incubations.
She smiles at that, acknowledges the snowdrops
still turning to the sun. *I'll have a month of summer*
she says, smiling. *About a month*
of summer.

Last light

They come softly, comforting, gentle,
carrying the wild chemicals
in their thin expensive cages.
Each syringe seems bloated, fat,
yet still too small
to hold such vast forces.

Fear hunkers down, spreads itself like oil,
her veins cord arms of faded bone,
her ancient eyes are holes where terror
sets its goblin mark.

She tells me how once, she visited Iona,
and would return. The island
enters the room like a boat; so
we hear the soft plash of water on wood,
understand sea-blueness, sea-murmur,
salt wind

and she steps inside thankfully, lifts her face
to evening over the long silver ocean,
allowing last light and the tide
to carry her through.

Birth

When the miracle comes in, world goes on.
Wards continue to be painted magnolia,
thin white plastics still shiver,
minstrel numbers continue to be counted.

When the miracle comes in,
blood locates its own new river
 – *all these sudden chasms and chicanes* –
but heart lurches forever, is stunned
by its sonic beating, repeating
the song of immense wings: swan
or crane or angel turning for home.

Around the miracle, unseen space
fills with colour so vivid a transfusion
that it sparks liquids and metals and skin;
even the distant sun at midnight flares
a greeting, extending long arms to wrap
new life in ordinary universal light.

First sun and daffodils

Always such a promise, a yes to life:
Sun's clear face open with warmth,
her hands bringing gold out
of black ground to kindle the shadows
left lying around under thin hedges
when Old Night stalked away.

A guinea morning.
Warm coin in cold pockets
and daffodils worth their weight
for all the singing gold they do,
taking up their places in hearts and borders
like blackbirds perched on twigs,
yellow mouths trumpeting the sun;

a sudden lightening of the spirit,
an old coat slipping to the floor.

When there is a word for joy

Sometimes, a man or a woman
comes skimming by,
their eyes like brilliants,
their hands loose and body loose, flowing,
skimming, mouths tilted upwards on a word
that mentions joy. The word
could be *cure*, or *birth*, or *remission*,
it could be *operable*, or *going home,* or *cyst*
or *sprain* or *virus* or the name of love;
their mouths shape round the word loosely
as if it was *sweetapple, peachslice*
or nothing remotely known in all the life
that had gone before: *green crystalline*
angelica, dark comfits of cardamom, wine
from grapes of Eden grown at Heaven's Gate
but whatever their word is, we understand it
as our own desire and hope, and we want
its diamond shining reflected in our own eyes.

Oversteps Books Ltd

The Oversteps list includes books by the following poets:

David Grubb, Giles Goodland, Alex Smith, Will Daunt, Patricia Bishop, Christopher Cook, Jan Farquarson, Charles Hadfield, Mandy Pannett, Doris Hulme, James Cole, Helen Kitson, Bill Headdon, Avril Bruton, Marianne Larsen, Anne Lewis-Smith, Mary Maher, Genista Lewes, Miriam Darlington, Anne Born, Glen Phillips, Rebecca Gethin, W H Petty, Melanie Penycate, Andrew Nightingale, Caroline Carver, John Stuart, Rose Cook, Jenny Hope, Hilary Elfick, Jennie Osborne, Anne Stewart, Oz Hardwick, Angela Stoner, Terry Gifford, Michael Swan, Denise Bennett, Maggie Butt, Anthony Watts, Joan McGavin, Robert Stein, Graham High, Ross Cogan, Ann Kelley, A C Clarke, Diane Tang, Susan Taylor, R V Bailey, John Daniel, Alwyn Marriage, Simon Williams, Kathleen Kummer, Jean Atkin, Charles Bennett, Elisabeth Rowe, Marie Marshall, Ken Head, Robert Cole, Cora Greenhill, John Torrance, Michael Bayley, Christopher North, Simon Richey, Lynn Roberts, Sue Davies, Mark Totterdell, Michael Thomas, Ann Segrave and Helen Overell.

For details of all these books, information about Oversteps and up-to-date news, please look at our website and blog:

www.overstepsbooks.com
http://overstepsbooks.wordpress.com